Rotorua
Stories Behind the Scenery

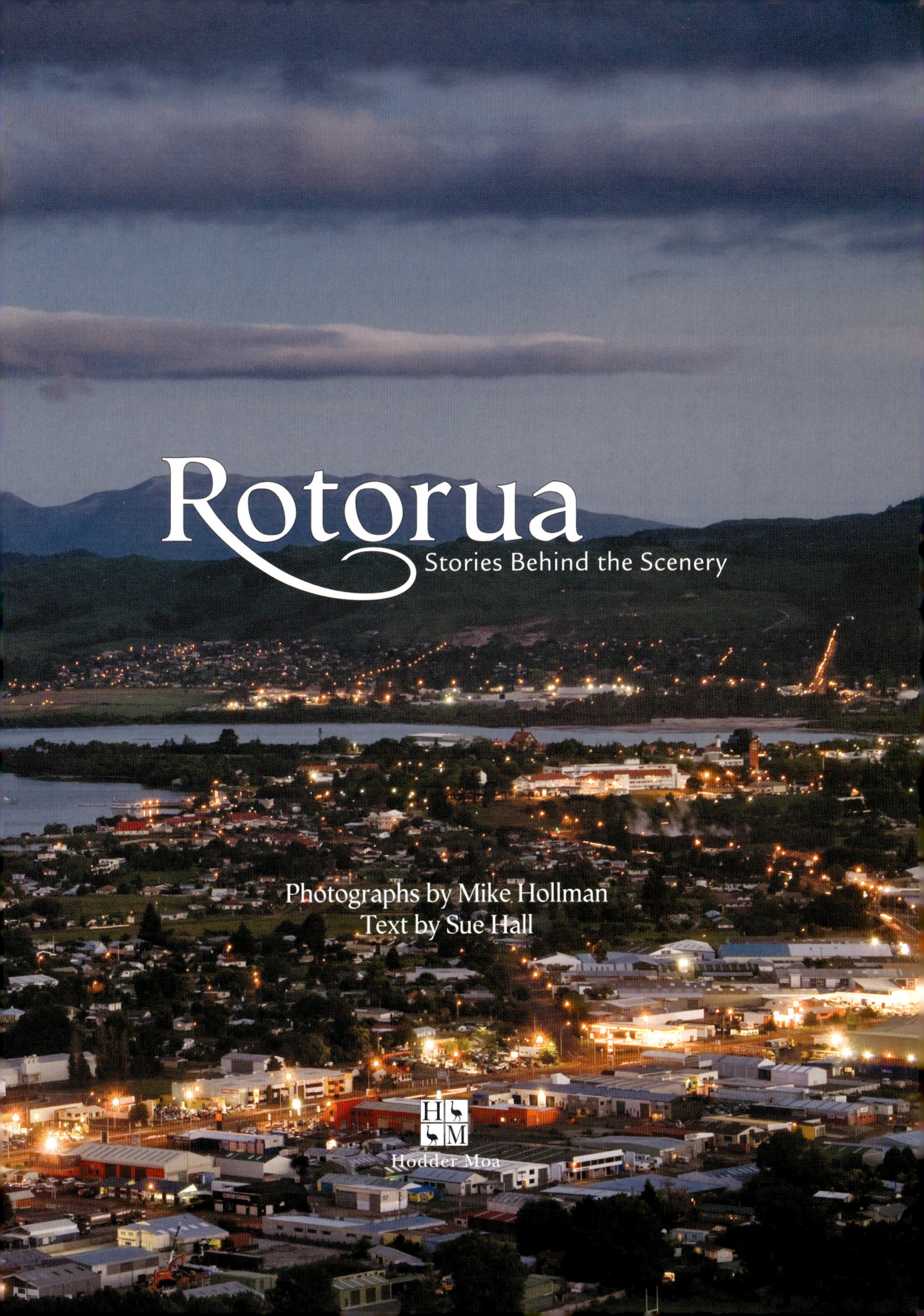

Rotorua

Stories Behind the Scenery

Photographs by Mike Hollman
Text by Sue Hall

Hodder Moa

National Library of New Zealand Cataloguing-in-Publication Data
Hall, Sue, 1951-
Rotorua : stories behind the scenery / Sue Hall & Mike Hollman.
ISBN 978-1-86971-164-1
1. Rotorua (N.Z.)—Description and travel. 2. Rotorua (N.Z.)—
Pictorial works. I. Hollman, Mike. II. Title.
919.342300222—dc 22

A Hodder Moa Book
Published in 2009 by Hachette New Zealand Ltd
4 Whetu Place, Mairangi Bay
Auckland, New Zealand

Designed and produced by Hachette New Zealand Ltd
Printed by 1010 Printing International Ltd., China

Front cover: Champagne Pool, Waiotapu Thermal Wonderland
Back cover: Fern in Redwood Grove, Whakarewarewa Thermal Valley; The Bath House in
Government Gardens; Maori cultural performance at Te Puia

Contents

Thermal wonderland

An Introduction

'Double bubble steam and rubble, geysers spout and hot pools bubble.'

If Will Shakespeare, in the sixteenth century, had even an inkling of the presence of New Zealand, and of the drama of its Rotorua region, the settings of some of the world's greatest literature might have been very different.

Te Arawa Maori, meantime, at home in their land of steaming surprises and boiling wonders — totally unaware of the presence of Europeans in the northern hemisphere — were creating their own rich stories and oral histories about their region and its people.

In Rotorua, near the centre of the North Island of New Zealand, steam rises from cracks in the pavements. Curious people lean over barricades around holes in public parks watching soft hot mud boil and bubble like thick soup. At several sites, geysers burst forth in violent steaming spouts. Visitors and locals lounge about rejuvenating body and spirit in natural hot mineral springs and thermal spas. Enigmatic pools display rich blends of vivid mineral-coloured whites, yellows, reds and oranges. Travellers

Pohutu Geyser, Whakarewarewa Thermal Valley

along highways watch wisps or clouds of steam rise mysteriously from within forested areas.

The outstanding geothermal attractions of Rotorua are world-renowned and, as a result, the region is the most visited tourist attraction in New Zealand.

Since the nineteenth century people from around the globe have flocked to see the curious natural phenomena of the Rotorua region and have been captivated by the natural beauty of the landscape. Forest, farmland and 16 navigable lakes offer peace, panoramic beauty and relaxation. Te Arawa Maori, tangata whenua (the local people), have always been willing guides, inviting visitors to understand and enjoy the land and its history, and participate in their unique culture.

Tourism has flourished and Rotorua city has prospered with it. A lively restaurant and café scene, varied accommodation, from backpackers to luxury lodges, specialty shops and well-organised tourism ventures and tours welcome a constant flow of visitors.

Whether seeking to experience awesome earth forces, Maori culture, rejuvenating spas or thrills and adventure, Rotorua has it all. The range of outdoor adventure activities is vast — including mountain biking, hiking, jetboating, luging, white-water rafting, paragliding, skydiving, bungy-jumping, trout fishing, boating, dragon-boating, four-wheel driving, volcano visits and scenic flights — based around the rivers, lakes, forest tracks and geothermal parks.

This is a land of geothermal wonders, astonishing visual medleys and rich mythology — a region whose vitality makes it one of New Zealand's 'must-do' attractions.

An issue of steam

The active Rotorua geothermal field is a visually astounding expression of the earth's geophysics. It comprises over 1200 geothermal features which include hot springs, mud pools, geysers and fumaroles, as well as silica terraces and flats.

The field is a major part of the great Taupo Volcanic Zone that reaches across the North Island of New Zealand — from the central Volcanic Plateau (around Mts Ruapehu, Tongariro and Ngauruhoe), across the Rotorua field and through the Bay of Plenty to White Island.

Because New Zealand lies over the convergence of two continental tectonic plates — the Pacific and Australian — many parts of the country have been stretched and strained over aeons, buckling and bending and responding to explosive pressure from magma (molten rock) within the earth. In several areas throughout the Taupo Volcanic Zone, magma has made its way nearer to the surface, close enough that it has become a geothermal heat source. When cold rainwater percolates down through cracks in rocks towards the heat source, it gets hotter as it descends. It then rises

Mud pools, Waiotapu Thermal Wonderland

quickly to the surface to discharge as geysers, fumaroles and hot springs.

New Zealand is one of only seven countries in the world that have active geysers. Through natural causes, and the extraction of geothermal steam to generate electricity, many of the world's geyser fields are in decline. Rotorua ranks alongside Yellowstone National Park as having one of very few remaining geyser fields.

Small geothermal systems exist throughout New Zealand, occurring at scattered hot springs in the Far North, the Hauraki Gulf, central Waikato and in the South Island. However, 80 per cent of the country's geothermal systems are found in the Taupo zone, the largest by far — and the most famous and spectacular — being the Rotorua field.

Volcanism has shaped the region too: the mountains and lakes of the Rotorua district are all the result of explosive volcanic activity.

Geothermal features

All the geothermal features of Rotorua result from the discharge of heated water and steam from hot rocks close to the earth's surface. Their amazing variety, across many different locations, depends on variations in pressure, temperature of the fluids, the composition and permeability of the host rock, the types of gas present and the age of the geothermal system.

The geothermal fluids that rise to the surface can be superheated water, water below boiling point, steam or mixtures of the three. A wide range of gases and minerals can also be emitted or precipitated during the discharge.

Fumaroles

Fumaroles are steam vents where water boils underground and steam is allowed to escape to the surface through holes or permeable

On the boardwalk at Waiotapu Thermal Wonderland

Lady Knox Geyser, Waiotapu Thermal Wonderland

rock. There is usually relatively little pressure associated with fumaroles, but the ground surrounding them is often warm.

Geysers

Geysers are formed when a pocket of groundwater accumulates and heats to boiling point. Large quantities of steam are produced. The steam pushes up out of the underground pocket, carrying water with it. As it rises the pressure is reduced so that more and more steam is formed. Once the surface tension is broken by increased pressure from below, the steam and water eject out at the surface in a steaming column.

Mud pools

Boiling mud pools occur in places where the base rock material is of a type that breaks down into mud, and where there is limited hot water but an abundant supply of steam. Hydrogen sulphide gas in the steam reacts with oxygen to form sulphuric acid, and this dissolves the surrounding rock into fine particles of silica and clay. When mixed with a small amount of water the heated gluey mix seethes and bubbles.

Steam vents, Waiotapu Thermal Wonderland

Hot springs

Geysers and hot springs function by the transfer of heat from brine, which is salty water deep within the earth's crust. When magma heats the overlying brine the hot brine carries heat upwards by convection; this heats the overlying fresh groundwater circulating close to the surface. Fractured, porous rocks allow the groundwater to flow to the surface, creating hot springs. Some hot springs pools are relatively passive while others release large quantities of gas. The peaceful rejuvenating spas throughout Rotorua are carefully selected for their health-giving minerals.

Silica flats and terraces

Silica flats and terraces are formed over tens to thousands of years as hot geothermal waters flow out, or burst out regularly, over the land. As the water cools it releases silica.

New Zealand had some of the largest silica terraces in the world. The famous Pink and White Terraces near Rotorua were considered to be the 'Eighth Wonder of the World' until they were destroyed by the eruption of Mt Tarawera in 1886. Other silica terraces and flats can be seen at Whakarewarewa, Waimangu and Waiotapu.

The Champagne Pool, Waiotapu Thermal Wonderland

Unique ecosystems

Adaptable organisms

Geothermal landscapes are far more than just visually fascinating features such as geysers and boiling mud pools. Their geological variety creates unique natural ecosystems which are home to many unusual plants, animals and micro-organisms, and to unusual assemblages of vegetation.

The micro-organisms found in geothermal water are believed to be closely related to the first organisms occurring on earth. They are known as 'extremophiles' because of their ability to survive in conditions of incredibly high temperatures and highly acidic water.

Okere Falls, northeast of Lake Rotorua

Other plants and animals in Rotorua show a fascinating resilience — a specially adapted leech lives in acidic waters and a low-growing variety of native kanuka tree grows only on the warm ground of geothermal areas. So special are some of the species of the Rotorua region that they have a number of potential uses in industrial processes, food and medicine.

The Waimangu volcanic valley, rearranged by the eruption of Mt Tarawera in 1886, is the world's newest geothermal ecosystem. A recent study shows that in this location native vegetation grows in unusual groupings. Stress-tolerant species that are also found in surrounding areas, for example, manuka and mingimingi, grow alongside fern or orchid species that are normally found in warmer climates.

Flora and fauna

Native trees, such as rimu, tawa, hinau, miro, manuka, cabbage trees, coprosmas and tree ferns, grace most of the bushland areas in Rotorua. The pohutukawa tree, a coastal species much loved for its Christmas-time crimson blossom, also fringes the Rotorua lakes. There are also several plantation forests of exotic trees, mostly conifers such as redwoods, Douglas fir and radiata pine.

Native plants, such as flax, kawakawa, titoki and various ferns, traditionally found everyday use for Maori who lived around Rotorua.

Flax was woven into myriad items, including mats, bags, clothing, bowls and rope (used for fishing and in the construction of shelters). Its sticky gum was used on sores and wounds because of the juice's antiseptic qualities. Almost every part of the flax can be used to make dyes, coloured from khaki, browns and pinks to apricot.

Tree fern in Whakarewarewa Forest

Kawakawa leaves were, and are still, used as a tonic and as a general drinking tea. The juice is said to settle an upset stomach and aid digestion. Chewing the leaves relieves toothache, and the leaves and bark made a poultice for wounds, ulcers and skin complaints.

Titoki leaves were prepared then boiled and rubbed on the skin as an insecticide. The

and the occasional kaka (parrot) or weka (woodhen). A great variety of plants and animals are showcased both day and night at Rainbow Springs in a lush native bush environment watered by crystal-clear mineral springs.

The lakes are home to a wide variety of water birds, from native species such as

Rainbow trout

red fleshy part of the root can be eaten.

The tender frond shoots of pikopiko (the common shield fern — also known as the native bush asparagus) can also be eaten.

Pockets of native bush in and around Rotorua and its lakes ring with the songs of tui and bellbirds and are peaceful havens for fantails, silvereyes, grey warblers, pukeko (swamp hens), kereru (New Zealand pigeon)

gulls, shags (cormorants), dabchicks and New Zealand scaup to introduced ducks and swans.

Rarer birds such as tieke (saddleback), kiwi, toutouwai (North Island robin) and kokako (wattlebird) can be seen in the sanctuary of Mokoia Island in the centre of Lake Rotorua.

The Rotorua area has 11 major lakes, along with many smaller ones, plus innumerable rivers and streams which make it one of New Zealand's prime trout fishing spots — practically guaranteeing a catch. As it is an offence to buy or sell trout in New Zealand, the only way to enjoy a meal of wild New Zealand trout is to catch one yourself (with a licence)! Many Rotorua restaurants will prepare and cook your trout for you, making the fishing experience individual and unique. Eels are also plentiful in creeks and lakes. Traditionally, local Maori prepared eels by smoking them, or by steaming them in thermal pools.

Kereru (New Zealand pigeon)

Kereru are plump native birds that early Maori favoured as a game bird. Protected from hunting since 1922, they remain at risk because of their rather ponderous weight which makes them easy targets for predators, and because of their low reproductive rate, breeding only when forest fruit is abundant. They eat the fruit of native plants and some introduced species such as privet, guavas and plums. When fruit supplies are low they will even eat the leaves of trees such as kowhai, willow and poplar.

As well as being visually splendid for their large size and striking colour, kereru are an essential part of the native forest food chain. Being the only forest bird large enough (since the extinction of moa — another large, but flightless, bird hunted by Maori) to swallow large seeds, they guarantee the spread of future generations of trees such as karaka, miro, tawa and nikau.

Weka

Weka, native woodhens, are part of the rail family, semi-aquatic birds that love to fossick near marshy areas. In the forest their main food sources are insects, lizards, eggs and fallen fruits, but they are also quite capable of killing and eating rats and mice, young rabbits and even the odd stoat.

Kereru

Weka

They are shy birds that are most often seen scurrying between one patch of vegetation and another or are simply heard rather than seen. Their numbers fell very suddenly between 1915 and 1940 in the North Island, with a large population remaining only in the Bay of Plenty and Gisborne areas. Numbers here have declined considerably since the 1980s.

Weka can breed all year round if the conditions are right, so it is possible to see a mother bird with both a juvenile and a chick in tow.

Tuatara

Tuatara are New Zealand's 'living fossils' — rare medium-sized reptiles that live only in New Zealand. They range in size from 300 grams to a kilogram (10.5–35 ounces).

Tuatara are of huge international interest to biologists because their nearest relatives, well-represented in the age of the dinosaurs, declined and eventually became extinct about 200 million years ago. Because they survive in the wild on only 32 outer islands, they are recognised here and internationally as a species that needs active conservation management.

Their aeons-old heritage makes them truly iconic creatures. Slow to do everything — breeding only every three or four years and taking 15 years to mature — if allowed to, a tuatara will reach the grand old age of 100 years or more.

Forest gecko

Currently there are over 90 species of lizard recognised in New Zealand, all unique to this

Forest gecko

Tuatara

country. Many geckos and skinks have unique features too, showing amazing adaptations to living in a cold climate, including being active during the day. The habitat of the forest gecko is in forest or scrub such as manuka where they hide under logs, stones or the loose bark of trees when not active. Although primarily nocturnal, they will sun-bask during the day, when they may change the intensity of their colours to blend into the background.

All lizards in New Zealand are protected and it is illegal to capture them or keep them in captivity without a permit.

Rainbow trout

Rainbow trout were first introduced to New Zealand in the 1880s and into Lake Rotorua in 1897. They are descended mainly from Californian steelheads — rainbow trout that migrate to the sea and spend most of their lives there. However, New Zealand rainbow trout do not migrate to the sea.

They are less widely distributed than the introduced brown trout, but can tolerate higher temperatures. For this reason rainbow trout, as well as brown trout, thrive in the lakes around Rotorua.

Enchanted land

Twenty-five generations ago the migration canoe *Te Arawa* arrived from eastern Polynesia. It explored Te Ika a Maui ('The Fish of Maui'/ the North Island) from Whangaparaoa (Cape Runaway) to Waitemata (the Hauraki Gulf) and made its final resting place at Maketu in the western Bay of Plenty.

As the Te Arawa people adapted to their new surroundings they moved further afield. Some explored the coastline, while others went inland searching for new places to settle. The tohunga (priest) Ngatoroirangi explored from Kawerau through to Tongariro. His travels had a lasting effect, and his story has been told through the years.

Ngatoroirangi and several companions struggled inland through dense bush. As they reached the centre of the island, clouds rolled away revealing the great mountain, Tongariro. Captivated by its splendour, Ngatoroirangi ached to climb it.

Taking his slave Aruhoe with him, he embarked on the climb — but not before telling the rest of the party to wait for him at the foot of the mountain and ordering them to eat nothing. The gods would then give the food's strength to him and to Aruhoe to help them in their climb.

The ascent was arduous and the higher the explorers climbed the stiffer their joints became in the cold. As they struggled to the summit the party below began complaining that they were weary and hungry. They discussed and argued their situation and eventually persuaded themselves that they needed to eat — after all, how were they to know whether or not the explorers had survived the climb?

As the party below ate, Ngatoroirangi and Aruhoe lost strength. They shivered and stiffened more, crouching miserably on the summit knowing they would die. In desperation Ngatoroirangi called to his sisters in his far-off homeland of Hawaiki asking them to send fire to warm him.

Carving in Government Gardens

The sisters heard his prayer and sent the fire goddesses Te Pupu and Te Hoata to find him. The goddesses swam swiftly. They surfaced at Whakaari (White Island, an active volcano in the Bay of Plenty), fire leaping around them. Realising they had a long way to go they submerged again and travelled westwards, surfacing again at Motuhora, Okakaru, Rotoehu, Rotoiti, Rotorua, Tarawera, Orakei Korako and Taupo, leaving cauldrons of fire in their wake. Knowing their time was limited they burst forth on the top of the pyramid of Tongariro — too late to save Aruhoe, but just in time to bring life-giving warmth to the tohunga.

And thus was formed the legacy of fire and geothermal warmth that still remains in the goddesses' tunnel between the Central Plateau, Rotorua and White Island.

Tangata whenua: the local people

For early Rotorua Maori, and generations since, the spiritual significance of their geothermal wonderland has been closely linked to its practical use. Settlements formed around hot springs where it was easy to gain warmth in winter months and where hot pools provided bathing and cooking facilities. The many lakes provided fish and the forests provided birds and edible plants. Gardens were developed on lake edges. Every lake, every mountain, every hot pool had its story. Every part of the life force had its spiritual or ancestral meaning.

Tribal groups of Te Arawa lived in villages scattered throughout the region. A generally peaceful life, however, was often punctuated by intertribal disputes. Many disagreements

A Maori cultural performance at Te Puia

escalated into full-scale battles, often exacting revenge for previous wrongs. Places of strategic importance were fought over (such as Mokoia Island in the centre of Lake Rotorua). Prisoners were taken and made into slaves. Rangatira (leaders) or relatives of rangatira were killed and eaten in revenge, often setting up reasons for further attacks. Warriors in each tribe remained aware of the possibility of attack so protocols of cautious welcome developed.

At other times marriages were forged to bring peace and reconciliation and to help lay claim to land use. Loosely, Ngati Whakaue lived on the western and southern sides of Lake Rotorua, Tuhourangi in the south-east and Ngati Pikiao in the east, but disputes among them and with outlying tribes saw changes of possession and occupancy over several generations.

Maori welcome

In the nineteenth century European tourists arrived regularly in Rotorua to experience the wonders of the geothermal landscape and the therapeutic spas. They were welcomed by local Maori who were helpful and gracious guides.

In particular, visitors came to view the Pink and White Terraces on Lake Rotomahana that were famed internationally. Massive layered silica terraces at two separate locations 1.5 kilometres (1 mile) apart on Lake Rotomahana held people's awe and imagination. Te Tarata (The Tattooed Rock) or the White Terraces was the larger. Covering nearly three hectares (seven acres), it tumbled to the lake from a height of 30 metres (100 feet), fanning to a frontage of 240 metres (790 feet). The terraces of Otukapuarangi (Fountain of the Clouded Sky) or the Pink Terraces, were smaller and lower.

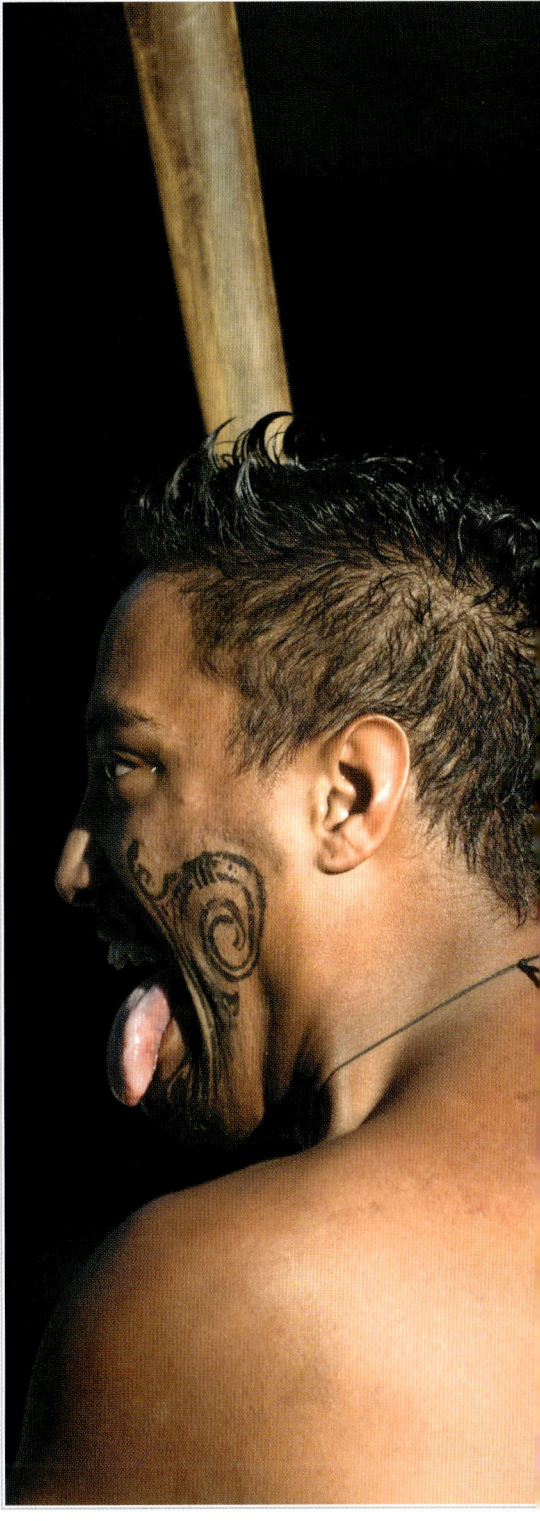

A formal challenge at Tamaki Maori Village

Tamaki Maori Village, Rotorua

In the late nineteenth century, tourist groups travelled by steamer to Tauranga and went by horse to Ohinemutu on the shores of Lake Rotorua. From there a coach took them to Te Wairoa to stay in the Rotomahana Hotel. From Te Wairoa, local Maori rowed them across Lake Tarawera in a whaleboat or small waka (canoe) 10 kilometres (six miles) to Te Ariki, from where they walked

and European settlers and the Crown (which engaged British soldiers) ultimately saw the confiscation of large tracts of the land of 'rebel' Maori. Little of the land of kupapa Te Arawa was confiscated. As a result, the tribal traditions and many of the settlements in Rotorua today hold and maintain an integrity that dates back 25 generations to the earliest of their ancestors.

Playing ti rakau (a stick game) at Tamaki Maori Village

3.5 kilometres (two miles) over the isthmus to Lake Rotomahana. They were paddled again by waka to view the terraces.

Because of this close contact with Europeans most Te Arawa were 'kupapa' (neutral in a quarrel) during the New Zealand Wars of 1843 to 1872. The conflict between Maori

The tradition of guiding and welcome for tourists that developed in the 1880s continues today. Maori in Rotorua are proud to share their culture and to impart the stories and arts that were learnt at the knees of their parents and grandparents and handed down through generations.

Lake Rotorua

Rotorua city

Rotorua city, which lies on the edge of Lake Rotorua, is a vibrant residential and holiday centre with a CBD of over 500 shops. Sixty restaurants or cafés cater for locals and visitors from around the globe. The city is famous for its parks and gardens which provide tranquil beauty for the 8000 visitors per day who stay here. Grand hotels from a bygone era and modern visitor accommodation vie with each other to provide the best and most attractive welcome.

Rotorua is 'the hub of Maori culture in New Zealand' — Maori make up 36.4 per cent of Rotorua's population compared with 14 per cent for New Zealand as a whole — and, for over 150 years, Te Arawa have welcomed visitors in a tradition called 'manaakitanga' ('caring for', 'showing respect', 'hospitality', 'entertaining').

Cultural protocols, warrior stories, myths and legends and modes of daily living are willingly shared with others.

Maori cultural centres are scattered throughout the city, some within original villages on geothermal sites,

Rotorua city view from the Skyline Skyride

Meeting house, Whakarewarewa
Thermal Village

where descendants of early Te Arawa still live. Some have been set up from scratch as business ventures showcasing Maori art and craft, cultural experiences and history. Everywhere, the city is alive with examples of traditional and modern Maori art.

Te Whakarewarewa Valley

The people of Tuhourangi/Ngati Wahiao have lived in and around the geothermal activity of Te Whakarewarewa Valley for over 200 years. Gradually, their valley became encompassed by Rotorua city as it expanded, so they now find themselves within the central city bounds.

Whakarewarewa Village and the geothermal field are entered through memorial gates and over the penny divers' bridge. This bridge has been a draw card for decades as village boys jump off to retrieve coins thrown into the river by amused tourists.

In the living village, where residents go about their daily business, manuhiri (visitors) can watch local people cook food in the hot water pools or taste corn that has been suspended in the water in muslin bags. The long history of guiding continues in the village and visitors can walk among the houses and hear the individual stories of the 189 pools — stories of love and loss, life force and spirit, conquest and myth — and then wander among the sinter terraces and geysers of the valley.

Tourism income is part of the lifeblood of this village so residents are more than happy to share their space. The role of the manuhiri is essential to the continuation of a traditional way of life within the village because the funds generated by admission fees and the sale of souvenirs are channelled back into the community in the form of maintenance of buildings, education and scholarships for the young, and welfare trusts for the ongoing well-being of all residents.

After closing hours the villagers can enjoy a quieter private life. Older folk still cook their dinners in steam boxes on a regular basis, first putting in vegetables such as potatoes, kumara and pumpkin. They come down later in the day to check their kai (food) and add greens such as cabbage, watercress or puha (sow thistle).

The most important building of the marae (gathering place) is the whare tipuna (ancestral house). It is also called the whare whakairo (carved house), whare nui (great house), whare hui (meeting house), whare puni (sleeping house) or whare runanga (council house), which demonstrates that this is the place where everything of consequence to the iwi (tribe), hapu (subtribe) or whanau (family) takes place.

Named after the ancestor Wahiao — the rangatira who first developed the Te Puia pa (fort, village) on the hill behind the valley — the meeting house represents the ancestor's body. The tekoteko figure on the top protects the great house, the koruru (carved face) is the head of the ancestor, and the maihi (bargeboards) stretch out like arms over the amo (upright support posts). On the ends of the maihi are the raparapa which represent the fingers of the ancestor. The tahuhu (ridgepole) which runs the length of the house inside is considered to be his backbone or spine, and the heke (rafters) are his ribs. The inside of the great house is his belly.

The walls inside are an archive of the tribe, the carved and woven wall panels recording priceless history.

Boiling mineral springs at Whakarewarewa Thermal Village

Gateway to Te Puia

Te Puia

When Sir Apirana Ngata (Member of Parliament) sought to revive Maori carving in the 1920s, he turned to a generation of Ngati Tarawhai carvers from Rotoiti. Interest grew and in 1927 the School of Maori Arts and Crafts opened at Whakarewarewa. Recognising the struggles of Maori to maintain their culture, the government passed legislation in 1963 to encourage, foster and restore Maori culture, arts and crafts, and to train students and exhibit works. In 1967, the first carving intake entered the New Zealand Maori Arts and Crafts Institute in Te Whakarewarewa

Geothermal Valley reserve.

The institute is now part of Te Puia, a thriving cultural centre where Maori are kaitiaki (guardians) of the geothermal resource and of their cultural heritage. Dramatic entry gates of modern design welcome manuhiri to the geothermal valley and to the institute.

Demonstrations of carving and weaving skills, kapa haka (action songs) and traditional games, storytelling and re-enactments of history and mythology occur regularly here throughout the day and evening.

The model pa at Rotowhio marae shows off the traditional carving skills of students. The whare nui, built by students of the carving school, and taking 10 years to complete, was opened in

Carving at Te Puia

1981. One of the most intricate structures on the marae is the pataka, a small, richly carved storehouse — used to safeguard the heirlooms and treasures of ariki (chiefs) and rangatira. Exciting modern woven and carved structures and designs are also showcased throughout the centre.

The name Te Puia represents the valley and a strategic pa overlooking the valley that was first occupied around AD 1325. Built on a rise beneath the cliffs of Pohaturoa Mountain, it was surrounded by a lethal moat of steaming pools. Palisade walls were built with a gap near ground level so the Te Puia warriors could slice the legs off anyone trying to scale them. Thus the fortress — which housed the women and children as well as the warriors in times of battle — was impenetrable. It was the only stronghold in the region to consistently resist invasion.

Te Puia, the cultural centre, is seen as a bastion of culture, protecting and preserving traditions and new art, conserving history, encouraging understanding and making a way for the future.

Pohutu Geyser

In the Whakarewarewa Valley some 500 pools and at least 65 geyser vents each have their own name. Seven geysers are active and the most famous, Pohutu — meaning big splash or explosion — can erupt up to 30 metres (100 feet) high, depending on its mood.

The activity of each geyser is affected by that of those nearby, as pressure waxes and wanes. As the guides tell their visitors, the geysers have good days and bad days.

A cause of great consternation in the 1970s and 80s, the good days became few and far between. Increased withdrawal of heat from the geothermal reserves throughout the city for heating and spa pools led to reduced pressure. Pohutu languished, guides worried and tourists

Pohutu Geyser, Whakarewarewa Thermal Valley

were disappointed. So the government stepped in and (controversially) restricted users from taking energy from the field. Now Pohutu bursts into life about 20 times a day.

Tourist guides

The long tradition of guiding in the Rotorua area has brought forth some personalities of international renown. Alfred Warbrick, one of the first guides, was particularly active after the 1886 eruption of Mt Tarawera, followed by Sophia Hinerangi, who also saw the eruption.

Possibly best known were Makereti Papakura (Guide Maggie), who performed a similar role in the early 1900s, Rangitiaria Dennan (Guide Rangi) from the 1920s to the 1960s, and Dorothy 'Bubbles' Mihinui in the later twentieth century.

Guide Maggie came into the world as Margaret Pattison Thom in 1873, the daughter of an English musician (a scout in the Armed Constabulary) and a high-born Maori mother (from the Ngati Wahiao hapu of Tuhourangi and descended from Ngatoroirangi, the great tohunga who called up the fire under Rotorua). The Maori translation of her name was Makereti.

Because the descent line of her mother's family was dying out, Makereti's survival

Pohutu Geyser, Whakarewarewa Thermal Valley

was extremely important to the tribe. She was therefore taken to live with a great-aunt and great-uncle in the Whakarewarewa Thermal Village where she was taught the genealogies, history and customs of her tribe. Her schooling, which included tuition from an English governess, gave her the language skills and confidence to move easily between the European and Maori worlds.

Makereti became involved in tourism as a child. Some of her writings in later life state: 'In those days [the 1880s] the bridge across the Puarenga Stream was a footbridge. We charged tourists a toll of 3/- per person to cross the bridge and see the sights.'

The Tarawera eruption brought trauma to the community and tension between tribes when refugees from Tarawera flocked to Whakarewarewa. Tourism was sorely affected by the destruction of the Pink and White Terraces, but in the early 1900s Guide Maggie helped stimulate interest by organising action songs and concerts for tourists.

As Maggie Dennan (having married Frank Dennan, a surveyor, in 1891, in a marriage that lasted only eight years), Maggie continued her guiding career. She took on the name Papakura when a tourist insisted on asking for her Maori name. Looking at the nearby Papakura Geyser, she said, 'My name is Maggie Papakura.'

So, it was Maggie Papakura and Guide Sophia who were invited to guide the Duke and Duchess of York (later King George V and Queen Mary) in the royal tour of 1901, launching Maggie as the Maori postcard girl whose image was sent and taken to other countries. It was Maggie Papakura who took troupes of Maori to Sydney

and Melbourne. In 1911 she took a 40-strong Te Arawa concert party to England, where they performed at the Crystal Palace and launched a 14-metre (45-feet) canoe in the Henley Royal Regatta. She later married an Englishman and lived out her life in Oxfordshire.

Makereti (Maggie Papakura) took te ao Maori (the world of Maori) to the world and, in doing so, inspired more people of the world to come to Rotorua.

Rangitiaria Dennan (Guide Rangi), Makereti's daughter-in-law, began her contribution to the region's tourism in Whakarewarewa in the early 1920s. She also became a guide to many well-known international visitors, including royalty. A photo of Rangi with Eleanor Roosevelt, wife of the then United States president, made world headlines. In 1957 Rangi received an MBE, and accepted the honour in traditional Maori clothing. Afterwards she commented that she was probably the only person to attend a Government House investiture in bare feet!

Rotorua and Ohinemutu

Some five generations after the *Te Arawa* canoe finally came ashore at Maketu in the Bay of Plenty, a young man by the name of Ihenga went searching inland for delicacies for his wife. When his dog brought him a waterbird he went looking with interest and came across a lake. This lake he named Rotoiti ('Small Lake') — it lies to the north-east of

Rotorua towards Whakatane.

Upon further exploration Ihenga came across a second lake which he named Rotorua (rua means two). The abundance of natural resources — the many fish that inhabited the lake and adjacent streams, the birds that occupied the forests and the many varieties of roots and plants that were a large part of his people's diet — attracted him. Not only that, he came across hot springs and thermal activity that he knew would benefit his people.

After he returned to Maketu with news of his discovery, members of the tribe decided to migrate inland to the shores of Lake Rotorua. The hapu (subtribe), Ngati Whakaue, settled at Ohinemutu and their village flourished. Other villages sprang up around the lake and other hapu branched off to other areas. Ohinemutu, however, remained the main focal point for many years and continued to be so even after European arrival in the mid-nineteenth century. It wasn't until many years later that the government-controlled township of Rotorua superseded Ohinemutu in size and importance.

Today Ohinemutu is a suburb of Rotorua city, but the village retains a sense of spirit, history and importance. Like Whakarewarewa Village, it is open to visitors at all times — other than during special functions, such as hui (meetings) or tangi (funerals), when community needs take precedence over tourism.

Standing on the forecourt of the marae, as steam rises through the pavers from the earth below, you can feel the spirit and significance of this sacred place: its links to the ancestors and its importance to today's community.

The carving on the large meeting house is exquisite and highlighted by hundreds of shiny inlaid paua shells. Towards the lake's edge is the magnificently decorated Saint Faiths Church which highlights how Maori and European cultures have collaborated. Inside, century-old Maori carvings and woven panels add a unique dimension to the European Tudor-style architecture. The strength and intricacy of this artistry demonstrates the importance of this building to the early villagers.

The clever design of a window etched with

Sunset on Lake Rotorua

the image of Jesus clad in a Maori cloak makes him appear to walk towards you across the surface of the lake.

Mokoia Island

A boat tour to Mokoia Island in the middle of Lake Rotorua offers visitors the chance to hear the stories of its people and walk amid a bird sanctuary that is home to a number of endangered species. The island holds significance deep in the ancestral folklore of Te Arawa Maori. The following is their story.

There was once a beautiful high-ranking maiden called Hinemoa who lived at Owhata on the eastern shores of Lake Rotorua. Her father, who intended to arrange a suitable marriage for her, rejected the advances of many suitors.

At large intertribal meetings that occurred to discuss matters of tribal state, young chiefs and young men regularly fell in love with the legendary beauty. Some plucked up the courage to ask for her hand, but all were spurned and turned away by her father.

On Mokoia Island in the centre of Lake Rotorua lived a family with several

sons. The youngest, Tutanekai, had been born after his mother had an illicit affair with a man from another tribe. Her husband took the child in and raised him as his own.

Now, Tutanekai's half-brothers had all unsuccessfully sought the hand of Hinemoa, so when Tutanekai caught and held the glance of Hinemoa at a tribal gathering he quickly looked away. Someone of such lowly birth as his could surely not be of any consequence to her!

However, during several subsequent tribal meetings their eyes locked and each realised they were in love. All they could do was look longingly at each other and wonder whether their feelings really were mutual. One day, however,

they found themselves alone together for a short time — just long enough to proclaim their love and for Tutanekai to suggest to Hinemoa that she paddle across the lake to him one night.

'How will I know where to come in the dark?' she asked.

Tutanekai told her that she could follow the sound of his flute which he played every night. It was then that Hinemoa knew that the haunting melodies she had heard each night had been played for her, and her heart wept and leapt.

The next night, hearing the sound of the flute, Hinemoa crept down to the lake's edge. The tribal canoes were pulled up unusually high on the shore — too high for her to manage them into

A decorated fence at Government Gardens

the water on her own. She now knew that her father and members of the tribe were aware of her feelings for Tutanekai. Frustrated and crying, she had to give up her efforts to meet her love.

The next night it was the same story, and the night after. The canoes were pulled up high from the water. But, with the nightly serenade increasing her longing and urging her on, Hinemoa worked out a plan.

During the day she gathered together six gourds. Later that night she strapped three to each side of her body and slipped into the water. The swim was long and eerie in the darkness, but the sweet melodies of her love's flute guided her to his arms.

Hinemoa's valiant swim to her lover is now folklore, as her father, recognising the strength of her love, forgave her and welcomed Tutanekai's family as his own, thus forging new bonds and peace between the two tribes.

Government Gardens

The Government Gardens, on the lakefront in downtown Rotorua, occupy land that was once known as Paepaehakumana, a scrub-covered geothermal area with several therapeutic pools. The area was of great historical and legendary importance to local Maori for the many significant battles that took place there.

In the late nineteenth century, local Maori

Blue Bath House, Government Gardens

The Bath House, Government Gardens

gifted 50 acres of Paepaehakumana to the Crown 'for the benefit of the people of the world'. The scrub was cleared, topsoil was brought in for lawns and gardens, and croquet and bowling greens, paths and fountains and formal gardens were developed, all under the guidance of French-born engineer Camille Malfroy.

Oruawhata, a deep thermal pit of boiling water and poisonous gases — used as a burial site for the bodies of warriors, to make sure they never came into the hands of enemies — was filled in. Malfroy, an enthusiast for geothermal systems, used the steam to fire up artificial geysers whose pressure was controlled by opening and shutting valves. At the opening of the Malfroy Geysers, for the birthday of Queen Victoria in May 1890, water and steam leapt to a height of 12 metres (39 feet). Today the geysers are awaiting repair.

Several large trees remain from those early days of development, including an unusual Californian weeping redwood and multi-trunked Japanese firs.

Aiming to create a South Pacific spa, in 1908 the New Zealand government opened a large and elaborate bath house, built in the Elizabethan Tudor style of architecture. It complemented a sanatorium that catered for about 20 patients who came to 'take the cure'. Today the grand building houses the Rotorua Museum of Art and History and an award-winning exhibition about the days when people came from all over the world to 'take the waters'. So popular is it that two wings are currently being added to the building using original plans.

In 1933 the Spanish Mission-style Blue Baths became one of the first places where families could bathe together for fun (as opposed to the other purely therapeutic spas in the gardens). In the face of huge public protest the building was closed in 1982. It was restored and opened as a museum, tearooms and heated pool.

The acidic springs of the Polynesian Spa have long been used by Maori and Europeans. In 1878 when a disabled priest found relief there for his arthritis, they were called the Priest's Pools. In 1882 the Pavilion Bath opened there, to be followed by the Duchess Bath in 1901. In 1933 the site was upgraded and became known as the Ward Baths until 1969, when it was changed yet again to become The Polynesian Pools, and more recently The Polynesian Spa.

Today, the Government Gardens are a recreational park. The gardens boast a series of ponds, a border of immense azaleas, beds of annuals in spreading green lawns and an immaculate rose garden. It is also home to pétanque, lawn bowls, croquet, golf, tearooms and a band rotunda.

The wooden Prince's Gate arches at the entrance once spanned streets in the town to honour the visit of the Duke and Duchess of York (later King George V and Queen Mary) in 1901. After the visit, parts of the arches were moved to their present position. The elegant totara gateway has recently been fully restored.

Sculpture, both traditional and modern, adds dynamic interest throughout the gardens. 'Waitukei', a bronze sculpture by Lyonel Grant, was commissioned to mark the new millennium. It was partly inspired by the melding of Maori and European cultures in the

Prince's Gate, Government Gardens

area and deeply inspired by the ancestors and stories of the area. Some viewers see the male and female figures partly as an expression of the Hinemoa and Tutanekai story.

Lyonel Grant states that his aim, in the many media he works with, 'is to carry forward the mantle of Maori art using strong traditional values and disciplines, using new materials and themes'.

Possibly the best place to view emerging Rotorua art is at RAVE (Rotorua Arts Village), which is in easy reach of the Government Gardens. The complex — which includes Wohlmann House, built in 1908 for Dr Arthur Wohlmann, the first balneologist at the Rotorua Bath House — is a community arts centre which offers studios, meeting rooms, art classes and two galleries.

Outdoor ventures

Rotorua's geothermal attractions are enhanced not only by cultural interest but by outdoor ventures that offer visitors thrills, fun and excitement. Some are based around natural features of the area, such as the many lakes, rivers and mountains, and others have developed as a tourism offshoot of Rotorua's strong farming and forestry culture.

Skyline Skyrides uses the slopes of Mt Ngongotaha as the basis of its adventure and restaurant attraction. A luge track winds down the mountain at a scenic level. Another advanced-level track provides hurtling good fun — rest assured, the three-wheeled carts

The Luge at Skyline Skyrides

have a steering and braking system that affords riders full control!

The wide view from the Skyline Gondola, out over Lake Rotorua, the city and beyond, shows up the large areas of farmland and forest that surround Rotorua. In fact, the gondola itself travels over 36 hectares (90 acres) of redwood forest.

Forests

Much of the forest around Rotorua is native, but large tracts of land have been planted in exotic trees for the timber industry. Fortunately, not all plantations are destined to be milled. Several redwood forests that were planted in the early 1900s are now protected as recreational areas.

Timber milling began early in Rotorua and it soon became evident that resources would be exhausted if the industry had to depend on native trees. Experimental work with radiata pine began in the 1920s and, as the timber industry flourished, more land was planted.

Rotorua is now the centre of a significant log export business, mainly to key Asian markets. Because of its central location, much of the forest administration for the central North Island is based here. The world-renowned Scion research centre is located in Rotorua, as are a number of quality forestry-based educational institutions and consultancies.

The Waipa sawmill on the outskirts of the main urban area is the largest in Australasia. It has traditionally cut radiata pine logs from local forests and from the vast Kaingaroa Forest (New Zealand's largest exotic forest) to the south-east of Rotorua. With an area of 150,000 hectares (370,000 acres), Kaingaroa was, for many decades, the largest planted forest in the world.

Fern frond in Whakarewarewa Forest

Forest walking tracks

The forest heritage of Rotorua has seen many hectares of native and exotic forest — particularly around the edges of Rotorua's beautiful lakes — retained for recreational purposes.

The Department of Conservation has opened up many tracks for short walks or tramping. Some well-known short walks are the Blue Lake Walking Track, Hongi's Track and the Lake Okataina tracks. The Blue Lake Track is a 5.5-kilometre (3.5-mile) circuit track around Blue Lake/Tikitapu which passes through both native and exotic forest. Hinehopu/Hongi's Track travels 2.2 kilometres (1.3 miles) through Lake Rotoiti scenic native bush reserve to Lake Rotoehu — a pathway taken by Maori chieftainess Hinehopu around 1620 and by the northern Nga Puhi warrior Hongi Hika — when he portaged his canoes from Lake Rotoehu to Lake Rotoiti (and then on to Lake Rotorua) in 1823 to perform a surprise raid on Te Arawa people on Mokoia Island.

Lake Okataina Scenic Reserve, like many bush reserves in the area, provides a wealth of walking tracks from 'easy walk' to 'tramping' level. Scenic viewpoints and secluded tranquil spots by lake or river are ideal locations for a peaceful picnic.

Whakarewarewa Forest

The beautiful Whakarewarewa Forest is one of Rotorua's most spectacular assets, famous for its magnificent stand of towering Californian or coast redwoods. Only five minutes from downtown Rotorua, it was established in 1901 as a trial plot to test the suitability of different native and exotic forest species for commercial planting.

Dragonfly on a silver fern in Whakarewarewa Forest

A large tract (288 hectares; 710 acres), recognised for its diverse range of exotic trees and flourishing native undergrowth, belongs to the Rotorua City Council. Management of other parts has included deliberate strategies to welcome recreational users. As a result, some of the country's finest walking and mountain-bike trails — ranging from easy to challenging — can be found here.

The most popular of the walks is the

Redwood Memorial Grove track where you can meander through breathtaking redwoods (*Sequoia sempervirens*) on a soft underfloor of fallen leaves. These magnificent trees stand at approximately 60 metres (196 feet) and reach 163 centimetres (5 feet) in diameter. The Grove is dedicated to the memory of the men and women of the New Zealand Forest Service who died in the two world wars. A nature trail on another track identifies the different trees and shrubs.

In an area separate from the walking tracks, known as The Triangle, there is a world-renowned mountain-bike park. Two circuits, a BMX track and a labyrinth of custom-made single tracks, provide for both the faint-hearted and the gung-ho. Created in partnership with experienced mountain bikers, the trails have names such as Check It Out, The Tickler, Gunna Gotta, North Face and Be Rude Not To. Bikes can be hired in town and guided tours of the trails are available.

In the Whakarewarewa Forest Conservation Park — a section of native bush that borders the exotic Whakarewarewa Forest — is the Tuhoto Ariki mountain bike track. Starting at the highest point in the Whakarewarewa Forest (765 metres; 2510 feet), the track is named after the respected and feared Tuhourangi tohunga who predicted the Mt Tarawera eruption. Built by the Rotorua Mountain Bike Club, it is grade 3 in difficulty, meaning it has some excellent long downhill segments and the technical climbs of a true cross-country track. Linking Tuhoto Ariki with other tracks (such as Split Enz) can provide some of the best riding in the country.

Redwood grove, Whakarewarewa Forest

Agriculture

Early European travellers saw plantations of corn, melons, pumpkins and kumara (sweet potato) at Maori villages around the Rotorua lakes. Gradually, in the early nineteenth century, the landscape changed. Canterbury investors and settlers developed substantial flocks of sheep on the open land between Rotorua and Napier, and in 1910 in Ngongotaha the first butter factory was built.

Blocks of Crown land were offered to settlers south of Rotorua in 1928, and, at Reporoa, low-lying swamplands were reclaimed and turned into farmland. Farms were established where native forest had been cleared.

After the Second World War (and through to the 1980s) aspiring farmers continued to ballot for Crown-developed land, but it was only after aerial topdressing was introduced in 1951 that some farms on poorer soils became viable. New farming methods and the recent boom in dairying have led to tracts of plantation forest being converted to farmland.

The confluence of geothermal and cultural tourism with agriculture and forestry in Rotorua has spawned several agri-tourism attractions. Farmers and foresters, recognising the opportunities that the constant flow of tourists provides, have set up ventures that combine income sources. Just as Maori cultural ventures add excitement and variety to the city, so too do agricultural ventures such as the world-famous Agrodome, farm-stay accommodation and various other lumberjack and agricultural shows.

Sheep breeds on show at the Agrodome

Sheep dog demonstration, Agrodome

Agrodome

The World Expo 1970 in Osaka, Japan was where it all began. So successful was a show there produced by New Zealand's world-famous sheep shearer Godfrey Bowen, that he and Rotorua beef and dairy farmer George Harford got together to build New Zealand's first sheep-shearing venture for tourists.

A dome-shaped building to house the show was constructed on a 160-hectare (395-acre) sheep farm 10 kilometres (6 miles) north of Rotorua city. Ivan Bowen (five times world champion sheep shearer) joined the Agrodome team as senior showman and success was guaranteed. People flocked to the show, the business expanded and the venture won national awards, including the coveted New Zealand Tourism Award for New Zealand's Best Visitor Attraction in 1994. The show has now been introduced at several sites overseas, including Japan.

With an emphasis on audience partici-pation, the show introduces three audiences a day to the sweat and strains of sheep shearing. Nineteen sheep breeds walk on stage in formation, sheep dogs show their skill with sheep — and ducks! — and the audience has the opportunity to hand-milk a cow on stage and take part in a sheep auction.

Outdoors it's equally entertaining. A farmer's whistle and omniscient sheep dogs control small groups of sheep, guiding them through gates and patiently rounding them up when they break for freedom. The ever-watchful and obedient dog stares down the sheep to keep them stationary or runs to head them off and turn them around, precision and timing being the name of the game.

Currently, the New Zealand Agrodome is a working sheep and cattle farm with 1200 sheep and 120 beef cattle. It gives international and local visitors opportunities to buy quality woollen and farm products, a hands-on live experience of farming, and interaction with their commercially farmed animals such as sheep, goats, cattle, deer, alpacas and ostriches.

A sheep dog in action

Agroventures

In true Kiwi farming spirit, when a fire destroyed the Agrodome building in 1980, Ivan Bowen performed the show for his 100 guests on a nearby hill as the building smouldered. The setback was only temporary. A new building was erected and the business expanded to the point where now, within the Agrodome grounds, there is another attraction called Agroventures. Visitors can book in for adrenalin-pumping, self-powered, high-powered or gravity-defying adventures.

The Shweeb is a world-first adventure activity. A human-powered monorail racetrack consists of two overhead rail circuits, 200 metres (656 feet) long, that vary in height between two and four metres (6.5–13 feet) above the ground. Under the tracks hang high-performance pedal-powered vehicles or pods in which riders sit back in the recumbent position. Due to the minimal resistance, riders can pedal to speeds up to 45 kilometres per hour (28 mph) and, on the curves, at an angle of 60 degrees, making it a dynamic and exhilarating ride.

Pods can be joined together for tandem rides and between one and five pods can be loaded onto each track, enabling teams to race each other or race against the clock. The current world record is one minute flat for a

The Shweeb at Agroventures

The Swoop at Agroventures

The Zorb

600-metre (1968-feet) race and is held by a New Zealand male in the Under-25 age category.

Freefall Xtreme has people body flying on a cushion of air. A diesel engine, turning a DC3 aircraft propeller, creates winds of up to 180 kilometres per hour (111 mph), allowing punters to fly up to four metres (13 feet) high suspended on the tunnel of wind — the closest

jumpers take a leap of faith and rush towards the ground. Forestalling the inevitable splatter, the bungy cord is designed to return the jumper high into the air again and eventually to a soft landing.

Nearby, the Swoop has the ability to terrify up to three riders at a time as it propels them forward at 130 kilometres per hour (80 mph).

Freefall Xtreme at Agroventures

possible simulation of parachuting from a plane — but with a soft cushion to land on.

Those who are not 'blown away' by the Freefall Xtreme could always be lifted up the purpose-built 43-metre (141-feet) bungy-jump tower to be 'highly strung' on the bungy. Leaving behind a stunning view — over farmland to Lake Rotorua and Mokoia Island and down to the Ngongotaha River below —

Hoisted 40 metres (130 feet) into the air in a hang-gliding harness, it seems so easy to pull the release cord and soar. But soar quickly translates into 'rocketing' through space like a jet plane.

Yee-ha!

And, for turning turtle with excitement and not knowing whether you're down or up, a downhill tumble in the Zorb is a revolutionary experience. The 3.3-metre (10-feet) inflatable ball hurtles 150 metres (492 feet) downhill on the straight track at speeds up to 30 kilometres per hour (18 mph) and at a slightly slower, but totally disorienting, speed on the 170-metre (557-feet) zigzag track. Harnessed inside the ball, riders can choose to run 'dry and wild', or 'wet and wild' when water is added to the wash cycle.

Agrojet claims to provide New Zealand's fastest jet-boating experience. Professional drivers whip passengers around a purpose-built racecourse with acceleration of 0–100 kilometres per hour in under four seconds and cornering at maximum speed, creating four to five Gs. Harnessed, helmeted and protected within the boat's roll bar, passengers become one with the boat, glued to their seats — by adrenalin!

Natural playgrounds

The many lakes and rivers of Rotorua have inspired anglers, paddlers and boaties from early times. Guided trout-fishing safaris and sightseeing boat trips can be sourced throughout the region. Ten secluded bush-lined lakes offer both rainbow and brown trout.

The Kaituna River, which begins as the outlet of Lake Rotoiti, to the north-east of Lake Rotorua, is an ideal white-water playground for rafters, water sledgers and kayakers, propelling them over white rapids and dramatic waterfalls through bush-clad valleys.

Rafting on the Kaituna River

A 7-metre drop over the Tutea Falls on the Kaituna River

Tamaki Maori Village

The Realm of Tane/Tamaki Maori Village is another venture set up specifically to cater for tourists. Brothers Mike and Doug Tamaki made a leap of faith and defied the odds in 1989 when they and their families set up a pre-European Maori village from scratch 15 minutes from town, bought a 15-seater mini-bus and began a lively guided programme for visitors.

Winner of New Zealand's Supreme Tourism Award and four times winner of the national heritage and cultural tourism awards, the Tamaki Maori Village now hosts more than 100,000 people each year.

The road trip (originally seen by bankers as a deterrent!) is the ideal opportunity for an entertaining and humorous step-by-step introduction to stories, history and marae protocols before the visitors arrive at the village to take part in traditional welcome ceremonies.

Huge crackling fires burn in front of traditional whare (houses), the sounds of ancient Maori instruments echo through the bush and, at the heart of the village, cultural groups recreate traditions in performance, song and oratory. Carvers chip wood and women play traditional stick games. To top off the 3.5-hour evening experience visitors enjoy a hangi — a traditional feast of meat and vegetables steamed by heated stones within an earth pit.

The mellow, earthy and wholesome taste of hangi food remains as only one of many quiet and vibrant reflections on the bus trip back to the city.

Fireworks in the south

In the last days of May 1886 Maori and European tourists believed they saw a Maori war canoe paddling through the mists of Lake Tarawera. Many people corroborated the phantom sighting. The unknown canoe never made landing. Tohunga Tuhoto Ariki warned of impending disaster.

Eleven days later, on 10 June at 2 am, Mt Tarawera erupted, spewing scoria, ash and mud over the surrounding area. At Te Wairoa, 12 kilometres (7.5 miles) from the mountain, villagers were woken by a series of increasingly violent earthquakes. Explosions followed and people ran for cover wherever they could.

Terror reigned until the eruptions ceased by 6 am. Picking their way through the morning devastation rescuers and survivors realised their local landscape had been completely rearranged. Not a stick of vegetation could be seen for miles.

In one night's activity, the rising magma around and in the mountain had mixed with groundwater and lakes, turning the water into steam. Powerful explosions pulverised the land, blasting it high into the air as huge volumes of hot mud. The earth was opened along a

Carving at the Tamaki Maori Village

17-kilometre (10.5-mile) rift, splitting Mt Tarawera in two and exploding Lake Rotomahana to 20 times its original size. The famous Pink and White Terraces were completely destroyed. Seven craters had burst out in the area that today makes up Waimangu Volcanic Valley.

Five villages were destroyed, but at Te Wairoa only 15 were dead and many survived, huddled under stronger buildings. The survivors relocated to Rotorua. This was, and still is, New Zealand's deadliest eruption. The official death toll was 150, although the actual figure is now thought to be between 108 and 120.

Mt Tarawera

The eruption of Mt Tarawera happened more than 120 years ago. Now visitors can take a guided walking, four-wheel-drive or helicopter tour to the summit and gaze in wonder at the massive red, ochre and brown rift that split the mountain in two — a chance in a lifetime to feel and see the unimaginable awe and latent beauty of such forces.

Waimangu Valley

Another area greatly changed was the Waimangu Valley. Within 15 years of the Tarawera eruption, hot springs were established within the newly formed craters, making the area the world's newest geothermal ecosystem and, as such, a fascinating place to visit. The valley includes Waimangu Geyser, the world's largest, and New Zealand's largest hot spring, Frying Pan Lake.

The scenic bush cover too is relatively new and its adaptation to geothermal influences is a continuing subject of study.

Waiotapu

Waiotapu, approximately 20 minutes south of Rotorua, is the region's largest area of surface thermal activity and the most colourful. Wai-o-Tapu means 'Sacred Water', and it is easy to see why. Hot pools ranging in colour from rich green to turquoise blue, yellow and gold make a spectacular array. The colours are caused by mineral salts in the water, including arsenic, silver and gold.

Everywhere steam rises in wafts, creating an almost ethereal beauty. Along the edge of the Champagne Pool the spectacular colours are a magnificent example of the vibrant hues caused by mineral and silicate interference. A steaming waterfall spilling over from the pool comes to rest at the edge of one of the best examples of silica terracing in the southern hemisphere since the destruction of the Pink and White Terraces. A boardwalk allows people to get a close-up view.

In the Devil's Ink Pots the surrounding rock has dissolved in the steaming water and grey froth swirls in patterns over black water. Close by, mud boils in fascinating burps, plops and spurts, and over at the Lady Knox Geyser everything remains quiet until 10.15 each morning.

The timely eruptions of the Lady Knox Geyser were discovered in the early twentieth century by a gang of prisoners washing their clothes. The geyser erupted, shooting hot water 20 metres (65 feet) into the air after the men had unwittingly poured soap into the spout. The soap broke the surface tension on the subterranean water and released it in a glorious steam-driven spout. Now all it takes to get old Lady Knox firing from its white, conical mound of silica is a bit of soap every day at roughly 10 am!

The Champagne Pool at Waiotapu Thermal Wonderland

Rotorua facts

- The Rotorua geothermal field comprises over 1200 geothermal features.
- New Zealand is one of only seven countries in the world that have active geysers.
- Rotorua Airport is one of the busiest domestic terminals in New Zealand, with excellent links to all major cities.
- The town's accommodation capacity has increased from 452 in 1898 to 13,000 today. The city's attraction, locally and overseas, means that, on average, there are more than 8000 visitors per day staying in its commercial accommodation.
- In 1950, around 10,000 people lived on the shores of Lake Rotorua. Now the population of the main urban area is estimated at 54,800, with almost 20 per cent living in rural and lakeside areas.
- Including people of mixed ethnicity, the major ethnic groups in Rotorua District are European (72%), Maori (36%), Pacific Islands (4%) and Asian (3%). (Census respondents listed all the different groups they belong to, hence figures total more than 100 per cent.)
- The main industry sectors of the Rotorua region are tourism, forestry and wood processing, and agriculture. Horticulture, manufacturing, education, and research and technology ventures are also well established. Rotorua's central location is enhanced by highway access to the major export ports of Tauranga, Napier and Auckland.

Rotorua mean daily maximum and minimum temperatures

	Maximum (°C/°F)	Minimum (°C/°F)
Jan	23.0/73.4	12.7/54.9
Feb	23.0/73.4	12.8/55.0
Mar	21.1/70	11.6/52.9
Apr	18.3/64.9	8.8/48.0
May	15.0/59	5.9/42.6
Jun	12.0/53.6	4.1/39.4
Jul	12.0/53.6	3.1/37.6
Aug	13.0/55.4	4.4/40.0
Sept	14.7/58.46	6.1/43.0
Oct	16.7/62.1	7.8/46.0
Nov	19.1/66.4	9.6/48.3
Dec	21.1/70	11.4/52.5
Average	17.5/63.5	8.2/46.8

Mean annual rainfall: 1411 mm (55.5 inches)
Mean annual sunshine hours: 2119

(Source: www.metservice.co.nz)